HEAVENLY

ANGEL

LAY LAY

EXPLAINS

THE DIFFERENCE

BETWEEN A

'COLD CHRISTIAN'

AND A

'BACKSLIDER'

PUBLISHING COMPANY

ISBN: 978-0-6151-7483-9

www.crossover-ministries-publishing.com

TABLE OF CONTENTS

A 'COLD CHRISTIAN'

A 'BACKSLIDER'

JACOB AND RACHEL

BIBLIOGRAPHY

ABOUT THE AUTHOR

I was dedicated to Jesus Christ of Nazareth as an infant and accepted Him as my Lord and Savior around seven years old when a visiting youth group led me in prayer at the alter. During my Salvation Prayer I asked Jesus to use me in a special ministry. Something that very few other Christians would want to do. I saw all the people just sitting in the pews, the ushers, and the Sunday School teachers and realized any Christian could do that. I wanted something different. One day in church service there was a visiting minister at a church I was visiting as well. The Minister said, "Jesus is going to make you a 'Healer of a Heart'". Then he asked me if I knew what that meant. I said, "No." the minister said, "I don't either, but whatever it is, Jesus is going to use you in a powerful way.

Helping Rachael, Jesus showed me what a 'Healer of the Heart' is. During the course of me helping Rachael to the 'Promised Land', a real Heavenly Angel named Lay Lay and I were allowed one hour one day to talk about Spiritual and Family situations from the King James Version of the Word of God. These books are designed to answer a lot of Spiritual Questions not even your minister can answer or your Church Denomination. I know theology Doctors who can't tell you how people other than Noah and his family made it past the 'Great Flood', yet their names are listed in the King James Version of the Word of God right after the 'World Wide Flood'. These books explain that and much more. I have written these books to tell the whole truth about the Word of God no matter how difficult it may be for me or others. Yes, there are things I write in these books that I don't even like, but in all fairness and total honestly, I must say the WHOLE TRUTH. The title of this book is 100% real. HEAVENLY ANGEL LAY LAY explained to me the difference between a 'Cold Christian' and a 'Backslider'.

INTRODUCTION

We have all heard the scripture of the 'Hot Christian', the 'Luke Warm Christian', and the 'Cold Christian'. Everyone know what a 'Hot Christian' is. As many Christians I have talked to, no one could ever explain what the difference was between a 'Luke Warm Christian' or a 'Cold Christian', all they could do is quote the scripture. The first section of this book is about **THE DIFFERENCE BETWEEN A 'COLD CHRISTIAN' AND A 'BACKSLIDER'**. The second section of this book contains the good and bad times of Jacob and Rachel as a couple. All scriptures are taken from the King James Version of the Word of God. This book contains an excerpt from my book. MATTHEW'S WORD 'TWO':REAL WORD OF GOD BIBLE.

BOOKS WRITTEN BY WALTER BURCHETT, BA:

MATTHEW'S WORD 'TWO':REAL WORD OF GOD BIBLE   ISBN: 1-4116-6995-9

HEAVENLY ANGEL LAY LAY EXPLAINS WHY ADAM WAS NEVER CURSED
                    ISBN: 978-1-84728-176-0

HEAVENLY ANGEL LAY LAY EXPLAINS WHY ABORTED BABIES DO NOT GO TO HEAVEN
                    ISBN: 978-0-6151-7470-9

HEAVENLY ANGEL LAY LAY EXPLAINS THE BIBLICAL GROUNDS FOR MARRIAGE,
        SEPARATION, AND DIVORCE   ISBN: 978-0-6151-7481-5

HEAVENLY ANGEL LAY LAY EXPLAINS WHY PROFESSIONAL COUNSELORS HAVE 'HARDENED
        HEARTS'   ISBN: 978-0-6151-7482-2

HEAVENLY ANGEL LAY LAY EXPLAINS THE DIFFERENCE BETWEEN A 'COLD CHRISTIAN' AND
        A 'BACKSLIDER'   ISBN: 978-0-6151-7483-9

HEAVENLY ANGEL LAY LAY EXPLAINS WHICH BIBLE TO READ, WHICH BIBLE NOT TO READ,
        AND WHY   ISBN: 978-0-6151-7484-6

HEAVENLY ANGEL LAY LAY EXPLAINS WHY GAYS, LESBIANS, BI-SEXUALS, AND
        TRANSSEXUALS DO NOT GO TO HEAVEN   ISBN: 978-0-6151-7485-3

HEAVENLY ANGEL LAY LAY EXPLAINS WHY CHILDREN AND SPORTS ARE DEFINITELY A
        RELIGION IN TODAY'S SOCIETY   ISBN: 978-0-6151-7486-0

HEAVENLY ANGEL LAY LAY EXPLAINS WHAT 'MANY ARE CALLED, BUT FEW ARE CHOSEN
        REALLY MEANS   ISBN: 978-0-6151-7487-7

HEAVENLY ANGEL LAY LAY AND GUARDIAN ANGEL SHADOW GUESS THE REAL AGE OF THE
        EARTH   ISBN: 978-0-6151-7488-4

AN ABUSED MAN'S BATTLES, TRYING TO PROTECT HIS BOYS   ISBN: 978-0-6151-5191-5

HEAVENLY ANGEL LAY LAY

EXPLAINS WHAT A

'<u>COLD CHRISTIAN</u>' REALLY IS

The following is an excerpt from my book called, **MATTHEW'S WORD 'TWO':REAL WORD OF GOD BIBLE**. This is one of the Bible Mysteries Heavenly Angel Lay Lay shared with me on our way, taking Rachael to the Promised Land. Since a Heavenly Angel told me this, how can I change anything that any Heavenly Angel said and make it better? If you don't know who Heavenly Angel Lay Lay is or how I was allowed to work with three different Heavenly Angels, then you will need to purchase **MATTHEW'S WORD 'TWO':REAL WORD OF GOD BIBLE** and read it (ISBN: 1-4116-6995-9).   The first half of **MATTHEW'S WORD 'TWO':REAL WORD OF GOD BIBLE** is about how I was allowed to work with three different Heavenly Angels to begin with. The second half of **MATTHEW'S WORD 'TWO':REAL WORD OF GOD BIBLE** contains about 100 pages of Biblical facts Heavenly Angel Lay Lay was allowed to share with me. You will need to read the whole book in order to understand how I was allowed to work with three different Heavenly Angels for a little over a year of my life. Lay Lay explained to me why Adam didn't stop Eve from eating the 'forbidden fruit', what caused Cain to get so angry he killed Abel, what happened to the Raven from Noah's Ark and why it had to be the Raven that was let out first and then the Dove, how old the Earth really is, along with other Biblical Secrets that theologians and theorists do not know.

A REAL 'COLD CHRISTIAN'

I asked, "What about 'backsliders are they still Christians?" Lay Lay said, "Christians consider you a backslider even today, you are smoking, drinking, and you swear at times. Being a single male human, you probably lust as well. Yet you still have the power to order demons to Hell (Year 2000). You have talked to 'unclean spirits' and they know you are His child. For their theory to work and have Jesus not be able to use a willing vessel in His work is like saying the power of Jesus isn't strong enough to cut through all that sin to use a willing vessel when He wants to. Jesus uses Christians who sin because all Christians sin, Jesus also uses sinners when they are willing to be used by Him. Jesus used the boy living next to Clark and Deborah for Rachael to go over and kiss Clark, that boy is into Satan's Toys, you know the children's cartoon shows and video games that the characters get superpowers from because the character ate or touched something that gave them a super strength in one form or another. Jesus said, 'It's only a matter of time before that boy is possessed because he is playing with toys that are possessed by Friendly Unclean Spirits, children's play toys you see advertised on television all the time taken from cartoon shows the boy watches.

HEAVENLY ANGEL LAY LAY

EXPLAINS

WHAT A REAL

'BACKSLIDER' IS

WHAT A REAL 'BACKSLIDER' IS

I asked, "What is a 'backslider' then? Lay Lay said, "Christians have a misconception that if you sin again after you are saved you loose your Salvation, that's not true. There are ways to loose your salvation, but not like that. Everyone sins after they are saved; they may not know it's a sin, but they sin just the same. Just because a human doesn't want to accept a sin as a sin doesn't make it any less a sin. The Old Testament talks about backsliding when the 'hearts' of the people are saying 'no' to God. They are going back to Idolatry, worshipping another god, not accepting Jesus to begin with for the Israelites, relying on the Old Testament Covenant to get into Heaven, denying Jesus like the apostles did when Jesus was taken from them; they actually denied Jesus and said 'no' from their hearts out of fear of what would happen to them. Later, they all repented and it was after that Paul talked about a 'thorn' in his side, about sinning of the flesh, that's the difference between 'backsliding' and sinning from the flesh. Backsliding is saying 'no' from the heart (soul) instead of saying 'yes' to the Spirit of God, 'Fleshly sinning' is from the flesh. You want to say 'no' to the flesh, but your self-image isn't there yet, from your heart you always have a choice. From the flesh, you don't until your self-image gets up to where you can say 'no'. The healing starts in the heart where the spirit and soul is, then works it's way out through the flesh. Just like Detta when she told Jesus to leave, she was saying 'no' to Jesus from her heart (soul), so He left, when she asked Him to come back, He came back; this is her second chance. Detta will sin in the flesh and be ok, but if she ever says 'no' in her heart again it would be over if she were normal, since there are others in her, Jesus won't allow the others to suffer in Hell because of her stubbornness, that's why He said He would give the role of 'host' to an 'alter'. You have never said, 'no' to Jesus from your heart, you had so many elders in the church say you were going to backslide; you fell for Satan's trap, the elders in the church actually created the situation for you to start sinning again by the Power of their Tongue and speaking the situation into existence. In the Old Testament, God was talking to nations of people who had backslidden, like the United States and other countries today the heart of the people who are allowing all the man made laws to be above the Word of the Living God. God gave them several chances to come back to Him, He finally disowned them and gave the nation a Bill of Divorce then took the Children of Israel as His bride on an individual basis.   The saved spouse (God) is allowed to divorce the unsaved spouse (Anyone who does not want to serve Him.) if the unsaved spouse (Anyone who does not want to serve Him.) leaves the saved spouse (God) on their own and doesn't want to come back to the saved spouse (God).   Then the saved spouse (God) is no longer under bondage of the unsaved spouse (Anyone who does not want to serve Him.).   Like the United States and other countries today, the heart of the humans who are allowing all the man made laws to be above the Word of God, God gave them several chances to come back to Him.

In Proverbs 14:14 (KJV) the Holy Bible says, "The **backslider in 'heart'** shall be filled with his own ways and a good man, *shall be satisfied* from himself.
    Notice the verse says, **"backslider in 'heart'"**, not flesh.

    Usually when a Christian is first saved they have that joy in their hearts.   That would be like a Christian saying, 'Jesus leave my heart', I want to go back to where I was before, I don't want you in my heart anymore, if Jesus left due to sins of the flesh all the time, Paul would have been a backslider as well, because of that 'thorn' in his side.   Remember what Jesus said when Detta tried to commit suicide that whole week? Jesus said, "It's not good for a vessel to get too much pain and anger out at once.   It's worse to get too much out at once, than it is not to get enough out."   Jesus has to take His time removing the pain and anger in a vessel's heart, Christians want to work through their problems in their hearts, but how can they when other Christians and non-Christians alike are judging them so much, it's like pulling negative out of the heart and putting other negative right back in, it defeats it's own purpose.   That's why a lot of Christians stop going to church they get tired of being judged all the time, like you.
    Non-Christian counselors can't help a human, they don't even believe in Jesus who is needed to help heal a human's heart.   Non-Christian Counselors don't believe the problem is in the heart to begin with, they go by theories of dead humans believing the real problem is in the human's mind, but they don't connect the heart to the mind.

Christians Counselors can't even openly believe or talk about Jesus who is needed to heal the heart because of fear of either loosing their career, fined, or sued. You have backslidden in the flesh, but not in your heart, that just makes you a 'Cold Christian' instead of a 'Hot Christian', not a 'backslider' as the Word of God talks about, your flesh went backwards, but your heart hasn't, you have never disowned Jesus in your heart. You have been asked to leave a lot of public and private places because you started talking about Jesus. Jesus has always been in your heart ever since you asked Him to be your Lord and Savior. Jesus Himself doesn't even judge, that's the Father's job. The Father is the Judge; Jesus is the Intervener or Defense Attorney defending His Bride, and the Holy Spirit is the Comforter and Teacher. Are Christians better than the Father in Heaven or Jesus? That's where Satan made his mistake, he thought he was better than the Creator. How can the 'creation' be better than the 'creator'? The Groom is above the Bride, Jesus is the head of the house just like man is the head over the woman."

JACOB

AND

RACHEL

(CONTINUED FROM: HEAVENLY ANGEL LAY LAY EXPLAINS WHY PROFESSIONALS HAVE 'HARDENED HEARTS')

After I tell the reader Biblical Facts that Heavenly Angel Lay Lay told me when I was working with her and Shadow, I will be writing about different stories from the King James Version of the Word of God talking about the family aspects in the Word of God. How the different couples in the bible met, what the couples went through, and what men, women, and children are commanded to do and not to do according to the Word of God. Just like HEAVENLY ANGEL LAY LAY taught me how to do. This starts when Isaac and Rebekah are living in Beersheba.

JACOB AND RACHEL

Genesis 28:1-22

1) And Isaac called Jacob, and blessed him, and charged him, and said unto him, Thou shalt not take a wife of the daughters of Canaan (The wisdom Isaac had, he knew even though Rebekah and Jacob had deceived him and cheated Esau. Jacob still needed a good woman for a wife from the 'Proper Physical Bloodline'. Isaac was able to put his negative emotions aside and give Jacob proper advice concerning what Jacob needed to do and where Jacob needed to go to get a good woman for his wife).

2) Arise, go to Padanaram, to the house of Bethuel thy (your) mother's father; and take thee a wife from thence of the daughters of Laban thy mother's brother (Isaac

continues to tell Jacob where to go for a wife).

3) And God Almighty bless thee, and make thee (you) fruitful, and multiply thee, that thou mayest be a multitude of people (Isaac speaking into existence God's blessing for Jacob even after Jacob and Rebekah deceived him and cheated Esau);

4) And give thee the blessing of Abraham, to thee, and to thy seed with thee; that thou mayest inherit the land wherein thou art a stranger, **which God gave unto Abraham**. (Here is another confirmation that Abraham was the prophet, not Isaac or Ishmael)

5) And Isaac sent away Jacob: and he (Jacob) went to Padanaram unto Laban, son of Bethuel the Syrian, the brother of Rebekah, Jacob's and Esau's mother.

6) When Esau saw that Isaac had blessed Jacob, and sent him away to Padanaram, to take him a wife from thence; and that as he blessed him he gave him a charge, saying, Thou shalt not take a wife of the daughters of Canaan (Esau over-hears what Isaac blessed Jacob with which made Esau even more angry);

7) And that Jacob obeyed his father and his mother, and was gone to Padanaram;

8) And Esau seeing that the daughters of Canaan pleased not Isaac his father;

9) Then went Esau unto Ishmael (Remember, Ishmael is the son of Abraham and Hagar, the Egyptian woman, the daughter of the Pharaoh of Egypt, 'idol worshipping', non-Christian), and took unto the wives which he had Mahalath the daughter of Ishmael, Abraham's son, the sister of Nebajoth, to be his wife. Esau already had one wife, he had Judith the daughter of Beeri the Hittite, remember?)

Genesis 26:34, 35

34) And Esau was forty years old when he took to wife Judith the daughter of Beeri the Hittite (The same tribe who Abraham went to for Sarah's burial place), and Bashemath the daughter of Elon the Hittite

(Esau was still angry and became 'unequally yoked' with a woman outside the 'Proper Physical Bloodline', that make her outside the 'Proper Spiritual Bloodline' as well. That's why it was a 'grief of mind' to Isaac and Rebekah): (Esau married out of the 'Proper Physical Bloodline' even before Jacob and Rebekah tricked Isaac, for Isaac to bless Jacob instead of Esau even though Esau is the oldest son)

35) Which were a grief of mind unto Isaac and to Rebekah. (Esau and Judith are 'Unequally Yoked', they don't fit well in the marriage bond to each other. Now in rage and anger, Esau goes to Ishmael, the 'bastard child', that was born of Hagar, the Pharaoh's daughter, the Egyptian slave of Abraham and Sarah. Even though it was a custom of the land that Hagar became Abraham's wife when he had sex with her, God never acknowledged the marriage. The custom of the land never over-rules the King James Version of the Word of God. Esau goes to Ishmael for his wife on purpose, to get back at his parents, Isaac and Rebekah. Having sex with or marrying someone just to get back at your parents, or anyone else for that matter, is not the right thing to do. There is a lot of heart ache involved for all concerned when this happens).

10) And Jacob went out from Beersheba, and went toward Haran. (Beersheba to Shechem is 65 miles or 108.55 kilometers north. Shechem to Haran is 425 miles or 684 kilometers north. 65+425=490 miles or 818.3 kilometers south 490/25 miles per day=19.6 days/6= 3.3 weeks) (Merriam-Webster)

11) And he (Jacob) lighted upon a certain place, and tarried there all night, because the sun was set; and he (Jacob) took of the stones of that place, and put them for his pillows, and lay down in that place to sleep.

12) And he (Jacob) dreamed, and behold a ladder set up on the earth, and the top of it reached to heaven: and behold the angels of God ascending (going up) and

descending (going down) on it (the ladder). (This is the first time Jacob saw angels)

13) And, behold, the LORD stood above it, and said, I am the LORD God of Abraham thy father, and the God of Isaac: the land whereon thou liest, to thee will I give it, and to thy seed (God is fulfilling the promise He made to Abraham, not to Isaac or Jacob);

14) And thy seed (Proper Physical Bloodline) shall be as the dust of the earth, and thou shalt spread abroad to the west, and to the east, and to the north, and to the south: and in thee and in thy seed shall all the families of the earth be blessed.

15) And, behold, I am with thee (you), and will keep thee (you) in all places whither thou (you) goest, and will bring thee again into this land; for I will not leave thee, **until I have done that which I have spoken to thee of** (God won't leave Jacob until God fulfills what has been promised. There is one point here that needs to be brought up. God is allowed to leave once His promise is fulfilled).

16) And Jacob awaked out of his sleep, and he said, Surely the LORD is in this place; and I knew it not.

17) And he was afraid (feared, now why was Jacob fearful?), and said, How dreadful is this place (Why is a place God is at 'dreadful'?)! this is none other but the house of God, and this is the gate of heaven (because God said, 'until I have done that which I have spoken to thee of', meaning there will be a time that God could leave Jacob. God knew how Jacob bought Esau's birthright and how Jacob and Rebekah tricked Isaac into giving Jacob Esau's blessing and it was only a matter of time that Esau breaks free from Jacob's bondage and God wouldn't be with Jacob at that time).

18) And Jacob rose up early in the morning, and took the stone that he had put for his pillows, and set it up for a pillar, and poured oil (anointed the pillar) upon the top of it.

19) And he called the name of that place Bethel: but the name of that city was called Luz at the first.

20) And Jacob vowed a vow, saying, **If God will be with me, and will keep me in this way that I go, and will give me bread to eat, and raiment to put on,**

21) **So that I come again to my father's house in peace; then shall the LORD be my God** (Jacob is making a 'covenant' or 'deal' with God, accepting God as his God now on the condition that God goes with Jacob back to Isaac's house in peace. Before this time, God was not Jacob's God even though God was protecting Jacob due to the promise God made with Abraham. Just because the prophets had children, doesn't mean the children accepted God as their own God once they became at the 'age of accountability'. Just like today, a family may go to church and their parent(s) may be Christians, but that doesn't mean the children are Christians. Or the children may be Christians, but that doesn't mean the parent(s) are Christians. Heavenly Angel Lay Lay explains the 'age of accountability' in my book MATTHEW'S WORD 'TWO':REAL WORD OF GOD BIBLE):

22) And this stone, which I have set for a pillar, shall be God's house: and of **all** (This three letter word means **'everything'**, **including TIME**, not just finances) that thou shalt give me I will surely **give the tenth** unto thee (How many Christians tithe their time? A lot of Christians I have talked to go to church, attend special functions, but how much of the tenth of 24 hours a day, **each day**, do you spend in the KJV and in prayer or meditation (This means thinking about what the scriptures are saying)? Remember, Heavenly Angel Lay Lay said, 'the only real Word of God Bible is the King James Version, that's discussed several times in my book, 'MATTHEW'S WORD 'TWO':REAL WORD OF GOD BIBLE. Reading His Word and in prayer is tithing your time).

Genesis 29:1-35

1) Then Jacob went on his journey, and came into the land of the people of the east. (Rebekah is from Haran, remember?)

2) And he (Jacob) looked, and behold a well in the field, and, lo, there were three flocks of sheep lying by it; for out of that well they watered the flocks: and a great stone was upon the well's mouth.

3) And thither were all the flocks gathered: and they rolled the stone from the well's mouth, and watered the sheep, and put the <u>stone</u> again upon the well's mouth in <u>his</u> place (You notice the stone is literally called, 'his', a masculine term).

4) And Jacob said unto them, My brethren, whence be ye (where you from)? And they said, Of Haran are we.

5) And he (Jacob) said unto them, Know ye Laban the son of Nahor? And they said, We know him.

6) And he (Jacob) said unto them, Is he (Laban the son of Nahor) well? And they said, He is well: and, behold, Rachel his daughter cometh with the sheep.

7) And he (Jacob) said, Lo, it is yet high day (noon), neither is it time that the cattle should be gathered together: water ye the sheep, and go and feed them.

8) And they said, We cannot, until all the flocks be gathered together, and till they roll the stone from the well's mouth; then we water the sheep.

9) And while he (Jacob) yet spake with them, Rachel came with her father's sheep; for she kept them.

10) And it came to pass, when Jacob saw Rachel the daughter of Laban his mother's brother, and the sheep of Laban his mother's brother, that Jacob went near, and rolled the stone from the well's mouth, and watered the flock of Laban his mother's brother.

11) And Jacob kissed (Wow, love at first sight. Kissing someone you just saw without even saying 'hi'. They didn't start talking to each other until the next verse)

Rachel, and lifted up his voice, and wept. (There is one mistake that Jacob did compared to what the servant of Abraham did when the servant was sent to get a wife for Isaac. Does anyone know what that one, and very big, mistake was? Jacob didn't ask God for any sign to let Jacob know when the woman came that God wanted Jacob to marry, like the servant of Abraham did when he was sent to find Isaac a wife, remember? The servant of Abraham asked God for a particular sign from the woman, where Jacob is doing this on his own, not a very wise idea)

12) And Jacob told Rachel that he was her father's brother, and that he was Rebekah's son: and she (Rachel) ran and told her (Laban) father.

13) And it came to pass, when Laban heard the tidings of Jacob his sister's (Rebekah's) son, that he ran to meet him, and embraced him, and kissed him, and brought him (Jacob) to his (Laban's) house. And he (Jacob) told Laban all these things.

14) And Laban said to him (Jacob), Surely thou art (you are) my bone and my flesh (Laban's kin, relative). And he (Jacob) abode (lived) with him (Laban, Jacob's uncle on Rebekah, his mother's side) the space of a month (for a month, Rebekah's idea of a few days).

15) And Laban said unto Jacob, Because thou art my brother, shouldest thou therefore serve me for nought (nothing)? tell me, what shall thy (your) wages be?

16) And Laban had two daughters: the name of the elder was Leah, and the name of the younger was Rachel.

17) Leah was tender eyed; but Rachel was beautiful and well favored (Rachel sounds like a plateau, Satan loves deceiving in plateaus. Looks can be deceiving).

18) And Jacob loved Rachel; and said, I will serve thee (you) seven years for Rachel thy (you) younger daughter.

19) And Laban said, It is better that I give her to thee

(let you marry her), than that I should give her to (let her marry) another man: abide (stay) with me.

20) And Jacob served seven years for Rachel; and they (the years) seemed unto him (Jacob) but a few days, for the love he (Jacob) had to her (Rachel).

21) And Jacob said unto Laban, Give me my wife, for my days are fulfilled (Seven years had passed. Remember what Heavenly Angel Lay Lay said about periods? There is a span of time that goes by? Well, these scriptures prove that point, the period between 'her' in verse 20 and the word 'and' in verse 21 were seven years between the two of them. You can find out more about that subject in my book, MATTHEW'S WORD 'TWO':REAL WORD OF GOD BIBLE), that I may go in unto her (consummate Jacob's marriage with Rachel).

22) And Laban gathered together all the men of the place, and made a feast (A wedding party, some cultures still have this).

23) And it came to pass in the evening, that he (Laban) took Leah his daughter, and brought her (Leah) to him (Jacob); and he (Jacob) went in unto her (Leah).

24) And Laban gave unto his daughter Leah Zilpah his maid for an handmaid.

25) And it came to pass (later), that in the morning, behold, it was Leah: and he (Jacob) said to Laban, What is this thou hast done unto me? did not I serve with thee for Rachel? wherefore then hast thou beguiled (tricked) me (I guess trickery runs in that family)?

26) And Laban said, It must not be so done in our country (A custom of the land that got everyone in trouble. The custom of any land never goes above the Word of God or there is always trouble), to give the younger before the firstborn.

27) Fulfil her (Leah's) week (The wedding is to last a whole week), and we will give thee (you) this (Rachel) also for the service which thou (you) shalt serve with me

yet seven other years [The wedding ceremony continues for a week (Now this definitely reminds me of when Damien and Gabriella were married and their wedding ceremony lasted for a week. Damien 'prepares the way' for the Anti-Christ. That's in MATTHEW'S WORD 'TWO':REAL WORD OF GOD BIBLE. This subject is far too complex to get into in this book].

28) And Jacob did so, and fulfilled her (Leah's) week: and he (Laban) gave him (Jacob) Rachel his daughter to wife also. (Jacob got married twice in two weeks time to two different women)

29) And Laban gave to Rachel his daughter Bilhah his handmaid to be her maid.

30) And he (Jacob) went in also unto Rachel, and he (Jacob) loved also Rachel more than Leah, and served with him (Laban) yet seven other years. (You notice Jacob and Rachel married before Jacob served the second seven years)

31) And when the LORD saw that Leah was hated, he (God) opened her (Leah's) womb: but Rachel was barren.

32) And Leah conceived, and bare a son, and she (Leah) called his name Reuben: for she (Leah) said, Surely the LORD hath looked upon my affliction (broken heart); now therefore my husband will love me (In this particular instance God allowed Leah be become pregnant, but Leah was Jacob's wife first. However; this is the mistake of a lot of women even today whether they are married to the man, just living with him, or just his girlfriend. Women think that just because they get pregnant by a man they want to keep, the man will love the woman, the man doesn't, the man will despise the woman for the trickery the woman plays in getting pregnant in the first place and the man will love the child. What do I mean by 'trickery'? The woman tells the man she is taking birth control, or says she forgets to take a pill during a few days during the month, or it's

not her time of month yet and deceives the man, then she winds up pregnant on purpose. Condoms break so that's not a good option, the 'pill' doesn't work all the time, so that's not an option. The only good option is not to do anything until after you are married).

33) And she (Leah) conceived again, and bare a son; and said, Because the LORD hath heard I was hated, he hath therefore given me this son also: and she called his name Simeon.

34) And she (Leah) conceived again, and bare a son; and said, Now this time will my husband be joined unto me, because I have born him three sons: therefore was his name called Levi.

35) And she (Leah) conceived again, and bare a son: and she (Leah) said, Now will I praise the LORD: therefore she (Leah) called his name Judah; and left bearing.

Genesis 30:1-43

1) And when Rachel saw that she (Rachel) bare Jacob no children, Rachel envied her sister (Leah); and said unto Jacob, Give me children, or else I die (Rachel is blaming Jacob for not getting pregnant as if Jacob could control when Rachel becomes pregnant to begin with. Jacob was doing his part. Jacob must be getting really sore by now, if you know what I mean, two wives to satisfy. No wonder they all stayed in the 'Proper Physical Bloodline', I'd hate to think about what would happen if any type of Venereal Disease was introduced in their 'Proper Physical Bloodline').

2) And **Jacob's anger was kindled against Rachel** (If you think Jacob didn't scream and yell at Rachel, you're kidding yourself. How would you feel if you were blamed for something, especially something like this, you had no control over? I really can't blame Jacob. It's not Jacob's fault Rachel isn't getting pregnant, he keeps shooting, she just doesn't have the target in the

right place to be hit): and he said, Am I in God's stead (Am I God?), who hath withheld from thee (you) the fruit of the womb (Stopped Rachel from getting pregnant)?

3) And she (Rachel) said, Behold my maid Bilhah, go in unto her; and she (Bilhah) shall bear upon my knees (Have you ever pictured this in your mind? That would hurt, one woman kneeling down on the knees of another woman giving child birth), that I may also have children by her (Bilhah) (This is the same mistake Abraham and Sarah made with Hagar).

4) And she (Rachel) gave him (Jacob) Bilhah her handmaid to wife (Three wives, what a woman in anger won't do): and Jacob went in unto her (Bilhah).

5) And Bilhah conceived, and bare Jacob a son.

6) And Rachel said, God hath judged me, and hath also heard my voice, and hath given me a son: therefore called she his name Dan.

7) And Bilhah Rachel's maid conceived again, and bare Jacob a second son.

8) And Rachel said, With great wrestlings have I wrestled with my sister (Leah), and I have prevailed: and she (Rachel) called his name Naphtali.

9) When Leah saw that she (Leah) had left bearing, she (Leah) took Zilpah her maid, and gave her Jacob to wife (The sisters are still going at it against each other. Now Jacob has four wives according to the customs of the land).

10) And Zilpah Leah's maid bare Jacob a son.

11) And Leah said, A troop cometh: and she called his name Gad.

12) And Zilpah Leah's maid bare Jacob a second son.

13) And Leah said, Happy am I, for the daughters will call me blessed: and she called his name Asher.

14) And Reuben went in the days of wheat harvest, and found mandrakes (A Mediterranean herb used especially to promote conception) (Merriam-Webster) (Women,

this even tells you when the mandrakes can be found. During wheat harvest) in the field, and brought them unto his (Reuben's) mother Leah. Then Rachel said to Leah, Give me, I pray thee, of thy son's mandrakes (The women don't even consider the other children their own, even though they are supposed to be 'one flesh' with Jacob. That's what happens when you follow the customs of the land. Just like today, how many women fight each other and won't accept another woman's child equal to her own? I know a lot of women will say, 'I do', **'BULL'**, if it came right down to it they would choose their own child to live over another woman's child even if that other woman's child was the child of their own husband as well. I can just hear all the counselors say, 'Well, hopefully it won't come to that.' I'll tell you right now, I don't like the idea of putting my children's lives in the hands of the word, **'HOPEFULLY and no one will promise because they know they really don't know'**).

15) And she (Leah) said unto her (Rachel), Is it a small matter that thou hast taken my husband? (Now Leah is blaming Rachel for taking Jacob away from Leah. Sure does sound like men and women today finding out their boy or girl friend or husbands or wives are in an intimate relationship with someone else) and wouldest thou take away my son's mandrakes also? And Rachel said, Therefore he (Jacob) shall lie (make love) with thee (you) to night for thy (your) son's mandrakes (Now Jacob's services for the night are for sale between his wives, what does that make Jacob?).

16) And Jacob came out of the field in the evening, and Leah went out to meet him (Jacob), and said, Thou (you) must come in unto me; for surely I have **hired** thee (Hired? What does that sound like in today's terms? I wonder. Jacob doesn't even get the wages that were given for his services) with my son's mandrakes. And he (Jacob) lay with her (Leah) that night.

17) And God hearkened unto (heard) Leah, and she (Leah) conceived, and bare Jacob the fifth son.

18) And Leah said, God hath given me my hire (Paying someone for services rendered), because I have given my maiden to my husband (The sacrifices these women went through to give their husbands children and to have a family with their husbands. It's a woman's top priority to give their husband the most children, and to be the best wife to the man, of all the man's wives): and she (Leah) called his name Issachar.

19) And Leah conceived again, and bare Jacob the sixth son.

20) And Leah said, God hath endued me with a good dowry; now will my husband dwell with me, because I have born him (Jacob) six sons: and she called his name Zebulun.

21) And afterwards she (Leah) bare a daughter, and called her name Dinah (Rachel can't top a daughter, or can she?).

22) And God remembered Rachel, and God hearkened to (heard) her, and opened her womb.

23) And she (Rachel) conceived, and bare a son; and said, God hath taken away my reproach (Women actually felt unworthy to their husbands if the women couldn't bear children to their husbands. Now I know where Satanists get that concept, if the female can't bear children the female is 'dismissed' or 'killed', the female is not worthy to live any longer. I use the term 'female' here because Satanist girls in the Satanist Villages are not old enough to be called a woman, some aren't even in their teens when they first start reproducing. More about that subject in my book MATTHEW'S WORD 'TWO':REAL WORD OF GOD BIBLE):

24) And she (Rachel) called his name Joseph; and said, The LORD shall add to me another son.

25) And it came to pass (eventually), when Rachel had born Joseph, that Jacob said unto Laban, Send me away,

that I may go unto mine own place (back home), and to my country.

26) <u>Give me my wives and my children</u> (Jacob is ASKING Laban for Jacob's own wives and children. Apparently Laban has given Jacob a reason to be cautious about whether Jacob will leave with or without everyone and everything), for whom I have served thee, and let me go: for thou knowest my service which I have done thee.

27) And Laban said unto him, I pray thee, if I have found favour in thine eyes, tarry (linger): for I have learned by experience that the LORD hath blessed me for thy (your) sake.

28) And he (Laban) said, Appoint (tell) me thy (your) wages, and I will give it.

29) And he (Jacob) said unto him (Laban), Thou knowest how I have served thee (you), and how thy (your) cattle was with me.

30) For it was little which thou (you) hadst before I came, and it is now increased unto a multitude; and the LORD hath blessed thee (you) since my coming: and now when shall I provide for mine own house also?

31) And he (Laban) said, What shall I give thee (you)? And Jacob said, Thou shalt not give me any thing: if thou (you) wilt do this thing for me, I will again feed and keep thy (your) flock.

32) I will pass through all thy (your) flock to day, removing from thence (them) all the speckled and spotted cattle, and all the brown cattle among the sheep, and the spotted and speckled among the goats: and of such shall be my hire (Jacob would keep all the imperfect animals for himself).

33) So shall my righteousness answer for me in time to come, when it shall come for my hire (pay) before thy (your) face: every one that is not speckled and spotted among the goats, and brown among the sheep, that shall be counted stolen with me.

34) And Laban said, Behold, I would it might be according to thy (your) word.

35) And he (Jacob) removed that day the he goats that were ringstraked (marked with circular stripes) (Merriam-Webster) and spotted, and all the she goats that were speckled and spotted, and every one that had some white in it, and all the brown among the sheep, and gave them into the hand of his sons.

36) And he (Laban) set three days' journey betwixt (between) himself and Jacob: and Jacob fed the rest of Laban's flocks.

37) And Jacob took him rods of green poplar, and of the hazel and chestnut tree; and pilled white strakes in them, and made the white appear which was in the rods.

38) And he set the rods which he had pilled before the flocks in the gutters in the watering troughs when the flocks came to drink, that they should conceive when they came to drink.

39) And the flocks conceived before the rods, and brought forth cattle ringstraked, speckled, and spotted.

40) And Jacob did separate the lambs, and set the faces of the flocks toward the ringstraked, and all the brown in the flock of Laban; and he put his own flocks by themselves, and put them not unto Laban's cattle.

41) And it came to pass, whensoever the stronger cattle did conceive, that Jacob laid the rods before the eyes of the cattle in the gutters, that they might conceive among the rods.

42) But when the cattle were feeble, he put them not in: so the feebler were Laban's, and the stronger Jacob's.

43) And the man (Jacob) increased exceedingly, and had much cattle, and maidservants, and menservants, and camels, and asses.

Genesis 31:1-55

1) And he heard the words of Laban's sons, saying, Jacob hath taken away all that was our father's; and of

that which was our father's hath he gotten all this glory.

2) And Jacob beheld the countenance (attitude) of Laban, and, behold, it (Laban's attitude) was not toward him (Jacob) as before.

3) And the LORD said unto Jacob, Return unto the land of thy fathers, and to thy kindred; and I will be with thee.

4) And Jacob sent and called Rachel and Leah to the field unto his flock,

5) And said unto them, I see your father's countenance (attitude), that it is not toward me as before; but the God of my father hath been with me.

6) And ye (you) know that with all my power I have served your father.

7) And your father hath deceived me, and changed my wages ten times; but God suffered him not to hurt me.

8) If he said thus, The speckled shall be thy wages; then all the cattle bare speckled: and if he said thus, The ringstraked shall be thy hire; then bare all the cattle ringstraked.

9) Thus God hath taken away the cattle of your father, and given them to me.

10) And it came to pass at the time that the cattle conceived, that I lifted up mine eyes, and saw in a dream, and, behold, the rams which leaped upon the cattle were ringstraked, speckled, and grisled.

11) And the angel of God spake unto me in a dream, saying, Jacob: And I said, Here am I.

12) And he said, Lift up now thine eyes, and see, all the rams which leap upon the cattle are ringstraked, speckled, and grisled: for I have seen all that Laban doeth unto thee.

13) I am the God of Bethel, where thou anointedst the pillar, and where thou vowedst a vow unto me (God is reminding Jacob of Jacob's promise to God): now arise, get thee out from this land, and return unto the land of thy kindred (your kin).

14) And Rachel and Leah answered and said unto him, Is there yet any portion or inheritance for us in our father's house (Rachel and Leah has nothing left in their father's house)?

15) Are we not counted of him strangers (Laban doesn't see Rachel or Leah as his daughters according to Rachel and Leah)? for he hath sold us, and hath quite devoured (spent) also our money.

16) For all the riches which God hath taken from our father, that is ours, and our children's: now then, whatsoever God hath said unto thee (you), do. [Men and women, verses 4-16 is very important here. If you to re-read that and realize in verses 4-13, that Jacob, even though he is the head of the house, is informing both his wives, Leah and Rachel, what he is thinking about doing, sharing with them what God had said to him, and asking for their 'authoritative opinion' in the issue. (Guys, even though the 'final decision' is yours, you need to ask and take into consideration the 'authoritative opinion' of your wife'. You need to remember, that no matter what happens, good or bad, she is affected by all your 'final decisions' as well as you and any children in the situation. Do you see that? Women, I know this will probably be very difficult for some of you, especially the older women who have already had children. You have already lived through a lot of stuff the man hasn't even come across yet, but you still need to do as he says and when something does fail, even though you believe you can see it coming a mile away, you worked through a similar situation before, if you need to you can do it again even if you don't want to. I said, 'similar situation' for a reason. Women, in Psychology, there is a term called a 'variable'. I know you have worked through a lot with what you and the children have gone through, but with a man in the picture now, there is an 'extra variable', meaning the circumstances aren't the same any longer, and the

wisdom both the man and women bring into the relationship is also there, which creates an additional 'variable' as well. See the problem in the United States today? Yes, women have lived through a lot by themselves, but so have the men. If you have a man in your life now, he is the 'head of the family' according to scriptures. If he makes a mistake, over time and through good and bad time together, he will learn to listen to your 'authoritative opinion' more, especially **if**, and I say **if** because as I said, there are 'different variables' in the problems now, the man, the experiences, the ages of the children, all these variables have changed. The decisions the woman made with only her and the children at a young age are not always the same as the man, woman, and the children at a later age. Not only that, but the culture has changed as well, creating an additional 'variable'. So if the man finds out the woman is right, he will come to respect her 'authoritative opinion' more over time, but if the woman is wrong because of all these extra variables, he will take that into consideration as well. Women, Jesus taught you in certain circumstances, now Jesus has to teach you both in some similar circumstances, but also different circumstances. Some of the characteristics may be the same, while other characteristics are not.) In verses 14-16 Leah and Rachel are both answering the Jacob in the same way. They are both acknowledging Jacob's leadership and confirming Jacob's reasons to leave the country with all Jacob has, and without Laban, their father's consent or knowledge. In essence, they are standing behind their husband's decision along with their husband. They are no longer their father's daughter, but their husband's wife, they are 'one flesh' with Jacob]

17) Then Jacob rose up, and set his sons and his wives upon camels (Jacob had to have several camels, there were twelve children, and four wives and himself, not to

mention any other menservants or maidservants); (Now Jacob and his wives are heading back from Haran to Beersheba. Shechem to Beersheba is 65 miles or 108.55 kilometers south. Haran to Shechem is 425 miles or 684 kilometers   south.   65+425=490   miles   or   818.3 kilometers south 490/25 miles per day=19.6 days/6= 3.3 weeks)

18) And he carried away all his cattle, and all his goods which he had gotten, the cattle of his getting, which he had gotten in Padanaram, for to go to Isaac his father in the land of Canaan.

19) And Laban went to shear his sheep: and Rachel had stolen the images that were her father's [graven images, apparently Rachel was serving 'false gods'. Rachel may have been in the Proper Physical Bloodline, but she was not in the Proper Spiritual Bloodline (This is explained in detail in MATTHEW'S WORD 'TWO':REAL WORD OF GOD BIBLE). This is interesting, this may be another reason why God closed Rachel's womb for so long. Rachel was putting a 'false god' before God, where Leah wasn't].

20) And Jacob stole away (snuck out) unawares (unknown) to Laban the Syrian, in that he told him not that he fled.

21) So he (Jacob) fled with all that he had; and he rose up, and passed over the river, and set his face toward the mount Gilead.

22) And it was told Laban on the third day that Jacob was fled. (Jacob has a three day head start, that's about 75 miles or 125.25 kilometers)

23) And he (Laban) took his brethren with him, and pursued after (followed) him (Jacob) seven days' journey (It took Laban seven days to catch up with Jacob); and they (Laban and his brothers) overtook him (Jacob) in the mount Gilead. (Gilead is south, at least half and possibly two-thirds of the way back home)

24) And God came to Laban the Syrian in a dream by

night, and said unto him, Take heed that thou speak not to Jacob either good or bad. (The night before Laban overtook Jacob)

25) Then Laban overtook Jacob. Now Jacob had pitched his tent in the mount: and Laban with his brethren pitched in the mount of Gilead.

26) And Laban said to Jacob, What hast thou (you) done, that thou (you) hast (have) stolen (snuck) away unawares to me (Without me knowing about it), and carried away my daughters (Laban now calls Leah and Rachel his daughters, yet Leah and Rachel don't feel like Laban's daughters any longer), as captives taken with the sword?

27) Wherefore didst thou flee away secretly, and steal away from me; and didst not tell me, that I might have sent thee (you) away with mirth (treasures), and with songs, with tabret, and with harp (a feast)?

28) And hast not suffered (not allowed) me to kiss my sons and my daughters? thou hast now done foolishly in so doing.

29) It is in the power of my hand to do you hurt: but the God of your father (You notice Laban said, 'God of your father' and not 'our God'. Also remember, Rachel stole a 'graven image' from her father, Laban as well. Laban had fallen into 'idol worshipping'. Just like Jesus used Damien to get the girls back up to me on her way to the 'Promised Land'. Damien didn't have a choice in the matter. Jesus put His foot down and made Satan have Damien allow the girls to use his cabin (Satan's property) that belongs to Satanists, in Washington State. More about this in MATTHEW'S WORD 'TWO':REAL WORD OF GOD BIBLE) spake unto me yesternight, saying, Take thou heed that thou speak not to Jacob either good or bad.

30) And now, though thou (you) wouldest needs be gone, because thou sore longedst after thy father's house, yet wherefore hast thou (you) stolen **MY GODS**

(Laban knows about not only one 'graven image' missing, but more than one)?

31) And Jacob answered and said to Laban, Because I was afraid: for I said, Peradventure thou wouldest take by force thy (your) daughters from me.

32) With whomsoever (whoever) thou (you) findest (find) thy (your) gods (with), let him not live (die): before our brethren discern thou what is thine with me, and take it to thee (If there be anything here that is not mine, bring it before our brothers and let them decide). For Jacob knew not that Rachel had stolen them (the 'graven images').

33) And Laban went into Jacob's tent, and into Leah's tent, and into the two maidservants' tents; but he found them not (the 'graven images', 'false gods'). Then went he (Laban) out of Leah's tent, and entered into Rachel's tent.

34) Now Rachel had taken the images ('false gods'), and put them in the camel's furniture (the harnesses and saddles used on camels), and sat upon them. And Laban searched all the tent, but found them (The 'false gods') not.

35) And she (Rachel) said to her father (Laban), Let it not displease my lord that I cannot rise up (get up) before thee (you); for the custom of women is upon me (Talk about a custom of a land not being good. Here the custom of a land is used to hide 'stolen idols'). And he (Laban) searched but found not the images ('false gods').

36) And Jacob was wroth (angry), and chode with (confronted, argued) Laban: and Jacob answered and said to Laban, What is my trespass? (Jacob didn't use a normal tone of voice when he was balling Laban out) what is my sin, that thou (you) hast (have) so hotly pursued after (chased) me?

37) Whereas thou (you) hast (have) searched all my stuff, what hast (have) thou (you) found of all thy (my)

household stuff (that is yours)? set it (that stuff) here before my brethren and thy (your) brethren, that they may judge betwixt (between) us both (Who that stuff belongs to).

38) This twenty years have I been with thee (you); thy (your) ewes (Female sheep, especially when fully grown) and thy (your) she goats have not cast their young, and the rams of thy (your) flock have I not eaten.

39) That which was torn of beasts (The wasted meat that the wild animals killed) I brought not unto thee; I bare (took) the loss of it; of my hand didst thou (you) require it, whether stolen (Killed by the wild animals) by day, or stolen (Killed by the wild animals) by night.

40) Thus I was; in the day the drought (heat and dry land) consumed me, and the frost (cold) by night; and my sleep departed from mine eyes (loss of sleep).

41) Thus have I been twenty years in thy (your) house; I served thee (you) fourteen years for thy (your) two daughters, and six years for thy (your) cattle: and thou (you) hast (have) changed my wages ten times. (Why would Laban change Jacob's wages? Why would Laban have spent all Leah and Rachel's money? Need I remind everyone that Laban is Leah and Rachel's father? So why would he do such things against his own daughters and son-in-law? Laban is serving Satan now, that's why. Laban loves money and worships Satan through his 'idol images')

42) Except the God of my father, the God of Abraham, and the fear of Isaac, had been with me, surely thou (you) hadst sent me away now empty. God hath seen mine affliction and the labour of my hands, and rebuked thee (you) yesternight (last night).

43) And Laban answered and said unto Jacob, These daughters are my (Now Laban is claiming his daughters again, his grandchildren again and all his cattle again. Everything that Jacob has Laban is claiming again) daughters, and these children are my children, and these

cattle are my cattle, and all that thou (you) seest is mine: and what can I do this day unto these my daughters, or unto their children which they have born?

44) Now therefore come thou, let us make a covenant (an agreement), I and thou (you); and let it (the covenant) be for a witness between me and thee.

45) And Jacob took a stone, and set it up for a pillar.

46) And Jacob said unto his brethren, Gather stones; and they took stones, and made an heap: and they (Jacob and Laban) did eat there upon the heap.

47) And Laban called it Jegarsahadutha: but Jacob called it Galeed.

48) And Laban said, This heap is a witness between me and thee (you) this day. Therefore was the name of it called Galeed;

49) And Mizpah; for he said, The LORD watch between me and thee (you), when we are absent one from another.

50) If thou shalt afflict my daughters, or if thou shalt take other wives beside my daughters, no man is with us (We will no longer be friends. This agreement is between Jacob and Laban); see, God is witness betwixt (between) me and thee (you).

51) And Laban said to Jacob, Behold this heap, and behold this pillar, which I have cast betwixt (between) me and thee:

52) This heap be witness, and this pillar be witness, that I will not pass over this heap to thee (you), and that thou (you) shalt not pass over this heap and this pillar unto me, for harm (They will not come against each other).

53) The God of Abraham, and the God of Nahor, the God of their father, judge betwixt (between) us. And Jacob sware by the fear of his father Isaac.

54) Then Jacob offered sacrifice upon the mount, and called his brethren to eat bread: and they did eat bread, and tarried all night in the mount.

55) And early in the morning Laban rose up, and kissed

his sons and his daughters, and blessed them: and
Laban departed, and returned unto his place.

Genesis 32:1-32

1) And Jacob went on his way, and the angels of God
met him.

2) And when Jacob saw them (This is the second time
Jacob saw angels from God), he said, This is God's host:
and he called the name of that place Mahanaim. (This is
about nine miles east of the Jordan River, what part of
the Jordan River is unknown)

3) And Jacob sent messengers before him to Esau his
brother unto the land of Seir, the country of Edom.
(Now, let's not forget that Jacob and Esau were not
exactly on speaking terms when Jacob left, remember?)

4) And he (Jacob) commanded them (the messengers),
saying, Thus shall ye (you) speak unto my lord Esau
(Now Jacob is calling his older brother, Esau his lord,
the same brother Jacob and Rebekah had cheated Esau
out of Isaac's blessing); Thy (your) servant Jacob saith
thus, I have sojourned (lived) with Laban, and stayed
there until now:

5) And I have oxen, and asses, flocks, and menservants,
and womenservants: and I have sent to tell my lord, that
I may find grace in thy (your) sight.

6) And the messengers returned to Jacob, saying, We
came to thy (your) brother Esau, and also he cometh to
meet thee (you), and four hundred men with him.

7) Then Jacob was greatly afraid and distressed (Now,
why was Jacob afraid? Remember, God was only with
Jacob for a time, until Jacob accepted God himself.
Jacob isn't thinking that God will protect him now
because the point God promised to protect Jacob is past.
Not only that, but remember the blessing Isaac gave to
Esau, saying Esau will some day break the yoke or hold
Jacob has on Esau. Now that time has come and Jacob
doesn't know what is going to happen): and he (Jacob)

divided the people that was with him, and the flocks, and herds, and the camels, into two bands (There must have been a lot of people with Jacob, enough for two bands);

8) And said, If Esau come to the one company, and smite it (kill them) (Jacob is preparing for the worst), then the other company which is left shall escape.

9) And Jacob said, O God of my father Abraham, and God of my father Isaac, the LORD which saidst unto me, Return unto thy country, and to thy kindred, and I will deal well with thee (Now Jacob is reminding God what God's promise is to Jacob. We need to do the same thing at times. Does God forget? No, but He still likes us to remind Him of His promises to us):

10) I am not worthy of the least of all the mercies, and of all the truth, which thou hast shewed unto thy (your) servant; for with my staff I passed over this Jordan; and now I am become two bands.

11) Deliver me, I pray thee, from the hand of my brother, from the hand of Esau: for I fear him, lest he will come and smite (kill) me, and the mother with the children (all the people).

12) And thou saidst, I will surely do thee (you) good, and make thy (your) seed as the sand of the sea, which cannot be numbered for multitude (Reminding God of His promise to Jacob).

13) And he (Jacob) lodged there that same night; and took of that which came to his hand a present for Esau his brother;

14) Two hundred she goats, and twenty he goats, two hundred ewes (adult female sheep), and twenty rams (adult male sheep),

15) Thirty milch camels with their colts, forty kine, and ten bulls, twenty she asses, and ten foals (All this for a present to Esau. Now remember Esau married a Hittite woman named Judith and a daughter of Ishmael's named Mahalath, Mahalath was the sister of Nebajoth,

Ishmael was Abraham and Hagar's son, remember? Esau had two wives who were not of the 'Proper Physical Bloodline').

16) And he (Jacob) delivered them (The animals that were a gift to Esau) into the hand of his servants, every drove (layer) by themselves; and said unto his servants, Pass over before me, and put a space betwixt (between) drove (layer) and drove (layer).

17) And he (Jacob) commanded the foremost, saying, When Esau my brother meeteth thee (you), and asketh thee (you), saying, Whose art thou (The layers of animals for the gift to Esau)? and whither goest thou (Where are you going)? and whose are these before thee (you)?

18) Then thou (you) shalt say, They (the animals) be thy (your) servant Jacob's; it is a (they are a) present sent unto my lord Esau: and, behold, also he (Jacob) is behind us.

19) And so commanded he (Jacob) the second, and the third, and all that followed the droves (layers of animals and people), saying, On this manner shall ye (you) speak unto Esau, when ye (you) find him.

20) And say ye (you) moreover, Behold, thy (your) servant Jacob is behind us. For he (Jacob) said, I will appease him (Esau) with the present that goeth before me (Jacob), and afterward I (Jacob) will see his (Esau's) face; peradventure (possibly) he (Esau) will accept of me (Jacob).

21) So went the present over before him (Jacob): and himself (Jacob) lodged that night in the company (The present to Esau).

22) And he (Jacob) rose up that night, and took his two wives, and his two womenservants, and his eleven sons, and passed over the ford (Shallow part of a stream that can be crossed safely) Jabbok.

23) And he (Jacob) took them (Jacob's two wives and two women servants and eleven sons), and sent them

over the brook, and sent over that he had (All that Jacob was going to keep).

24) And Jacob was left alone; and there wrestled a man with him (Jacob) until the breaking of the day (morning).

25) And when he (the man) saw that he (the man) prevailed not against (did not beat) him (Jacob), he (the man) touched (supernatural power) the hollow of his (Jacob's) thigh; and the hollow of Jacob's thigh was out of joint (The effects of the supernatural power touching Jacob's inner thigh), as he (Jacob) wrestled with him (The man, actually an angel from Heaven. Jacob had to have been one huge and tall man, I remember Shadow, Rachael's 'Protecting Angel', standing in front of the Anti-Christ and **Shadow, in his true form, had to LOOK UP** to see the Anti-Christ eye to eye)

26) And he (the man) said, Let me go, for the day breaketh (dawn). And he (Jacob) said, I will not let thee (you) go, except thou (you) bless me.

27) And he (the man) said unto him (Jacob), What is thy name? And he said, Jacob.

28) And he (the man) said, Thy (your) name shall be called no more Jacob, but Israel: for as a prince hast thou power with God and with men, and hast prevailed (won).

29) And Jacob asked him, and said, Tell me, I pray thee, thy name. And he said, Wherefore is it that thou dost ask after my name? And he blessed him there.

30) And Jacob called the name of the place Peniel: for I have seen God face to face, and my life is preserved. (I wonder if Jacob saw God in color or in black and white. I couldn't see Jesus in color, but in black and white. Seeing Jesus in color was too much for my physical mind to handle, He was always in black and white and the hem of His Throne Room Robe always turned from color to black and white when the brightness and intense warm power is too much for my physical mind to

handle. His 'fiery red eyes', when Jesus got angry with Mandy, were in very bold color)

31) And as he (Jacob) passed over Penuel the sun rose upon him (Jacob), and he (Jacob) halted (Had difficulty walking, was in pain) upon his (Jacob's) thigh.

32) Therefore the children of Israel eat not of the sinew (A tendon or muscle) which shrank (make smaller), which is upon the hollow of the thigh, unto this day: because he (the man) touched the hollow of Jacob's thigh in the sinew (a tendon or muscle) that shrank (make smaller).

Genesis 33:1-20

1) And Jacob lifted up his eyes, and looked, and, behold, Esau came, and with him (Esau) four hundred men. And he (Jacob) divided the children unto Leah, and unto Rachel, and unto the two handmaids.

2) And he (Jacob) put the handmaids and their children foremost (Apparently Jacob thought the handmaids and children of the handmaids were less important than Leah and Rachel and their children), and Leah and her children after (Now we see Jacob still thought Leah and her children were less important to Jacob than Rachel), and Rachel and Joseph hindermost (Now the most important to Jacob, Rachel and you also notice that Joseph is the only child of the twelve that are mentioned here).

3) And he (Jacob) passed over before them(the rest of the family), and bowed himself (Jacob) to the ground seven times, until he (Jacob) (This reminds me of the servant who bowed down to me when Rachael was talking to the girl, this is in my other book, MATTHEW'S WORD 'TWO':REAL WORD OF GOD BIBLE after the marriage of Damien and Gabriella, the girl kept bowing before me backing away, realizing who I was and that I was the Christian man helping Damien and Gabriella. I think Damien gave me the title of

'Prince Extended' without my knowledge) was came near to his (Jacob's) brother (Esau).

4) And Esau ran to meet him (Jacob), and embraced him (Jacob), and fell on his (Jacob's) neck, and kissed him (Jacob): and they wept.

5) And he (Esau) lifted up his eyes, and saw the women and the children; and said, Who are those with thee (Jacob)? And he (Jacob) said, The children which God hath graciously given thy (your) servant.

6) Then the handmaidens came near, they and their children, and they bowed themselves.

7) And Leah also with her children came near, and bowed themselves: and after came Joseph near and Rachel, and they bowed themselves (Still Joseph is the only child mentioned in all this).

8) And he (Esau) said, What meanest thou (you) by all this drove (the animals) which I met? And he (Jacob) said, These are to find grace in the sight of my lord (Esau).

9) And Esau said, I have enough, my brother; keep that thou hast (what you have) unto thyself.

10) And Jacob said, Nay, I pray thee (No, I asked of you), if now I have found grace in thy (your) sight, then receive my present at my hand: for therefore I have seen thy (your) face, as though I had seen the face of God, and thou wast (you are) pleased with me.

11) Take, I pray thee (ask you), my blessing that is brought to thee (you); because God hath dealt graciously with me, and because I have enough. And he (Jacob) urged him (Esau), and he (Esau) took it (the gift).

12) And he (Jacob) said, Let us take our journey, and let us go, and I will go before thee (Esau).

13) And he (Jacob) said unto him (Esau), My lord knoweth that the children are tender (young), and the flocks and herds with young are with me (Jacob): and if men should overdrive them one day, all the flock will die.

14) Let my (Esau) lord, I pray thee (ask you), pass over before his (Esau's) servant (Jacob): and I will lead on softly, according as the cattle that goeth before me and the children be able to endure, until I come unto my lord (Esau) unto Seir.

15) And Esau said, Let me now leave with thee (Jacob) some of the folk that are with me (Esau) And he (Jacob) said, What needeth it? let me (Jacob) find grace in the sight of my lord (Esau). (Jacob left some of the people with Esau)

16) So Esau returned that day on his way unto Seir. [Now remember, Esau married two 'idol worshippers', and he lived in Seir. **Seir**, also known as Seire, Seere, or Sear, **is a Prince of Hell with 26 legions of demons under his command**. **He can** go to any place on earth in a matter of seconds to accomplish the will of the conjurer, **bring abundance**, help in finding hidden treasures or in robbery, **and is not a demon of evil but good nature, being mostly indifferent to evilness** (Now this definitely sounds like a 'Friendly Unclean Spirit', doing good instead of evil to lead a person deeper into the occult and Satanism. Just like the children's play toys Heavenly Angel Lay Lay was talking about. The Friendly Unclean Spirits and Regular Unclean Spirits playing around and making sure the Friendly Unclean Spirits always win so the parents will buy the children their favorite toy cartoon characters just like Heavenly Angel Lay Lay said). Seir is depicted as a man riding a winged horse, and is said to be beautiful.]

17) And Jacob journeyed to Succoth, and built him an house, and made booths for his cattle: therefore the name of the place is called Succoth.

18) And Jacob came to **Shalem, a city of Shechem**, which is in the land of Canaan, when he (Jacob) came from Padanaram (around Haran); and pitched his (Jacob's) tent before the city. (Jacob never made it back to Beersheba. Shechem is north of Beersheba along the

Jordan River about half way between the Sea of Galilee and the Dead Sea. Beersheba is west of the Southern end of the Dead Sea, so Isaac and Rebekah hasn't met Rachel or Leah yet. Shechem is just west of the Dead Sea)

19) And he (Jacob) bought a parcel of a field, where he (Jacob) had spread his tent, at the hand of the children of Hamor, Shechem's father, for an hundred pieces of money.

20) And he (Jacob) erected there an altar, and called it EleloheIsrael.

Genesis 34:1-31

1) And Dinah the daughter of Leah, which she (Leah) bare unto Jacob, went out to see the daughters of the land.

2) And when Shechem the son of Hamor the Hivite, prince of the country, saw her, he took her, and lay with her, and defiled (deprive woman of virginity: to be the first man to have sexual intercourse with a woman, usually outside marriage) (Encarta ® World English Dictionary © & (P) 1998-2004 Microsoft Corporation. All rights reserved.) her. (I've heard that Shechem raped Dinah, but he didn't there is no indication of a rape, taking Dinah without her consent. The way the scriptures that follow are reading, Shechem and Dinah both were willing to go all the way with each other. If there had been a rape, the talk wouldn't have been for Shechem to marry Dinah, nor would the scripture say Shechem, the Prince of Shalem, love Dinah and speaking kindly of Dinah.)

3) And his soul clave unto Dinah the daughter of Jacob, and he loved the damsel, and spake kindly unto the damsel.

4) And Shechem spake unto his father Hamor, saying, Get me this damsel to wife. (Shechem, the prince of Shalem, wants to marry Dinah. That would make Dinah

a princess. When a boy says that to his father and the
father is the king of a country, that boy could have any
pick of women in that country. Dinah would be a
princess over all the land, and eventually the queen of
the land. Does that sound like Rape? Not to me it
doesn't. It sounds like they started flirting with each
other, kissing, petting and things went too far, but they
were both consensual in the act)
5) And Jacob heard that he (Shechem, the prince of
Shalem) had defiled (deprive woman of virginity: to be
the first man to have sexual intercourse with a woman,
usually outside marriage) (Encarta ® World English
Dictionary © & (P) 1998-2004 Microsoft Corporation.
All rights reserved.) Dinah his (Jacob's) daughter: now
his sons were with his cattle in the field: and Jacob held
his peace until they were come.
6) And Hamor the father of Shechem went out unto
Jacob to commune (talk) with him (Jacob).
7) And the sons of Jacob came out of the field when
they heard it: and the men were grieved, and they were
very wroth (angry) (See, there are all kinds of people in
the Old Testament who got angry just like Heavenly
Angel Lay Lay said there were. It's not wrong to get
angry like a lot of secular or Christian counselors say or
teach, what is wrong is allowing that anger to go to the
extreme. What is an extreme? Using more anger and
force than necessary to get the job done when the job
could have been done with less force. How can you
tell? Each situation and group of people or couples in a
marriage or relationship is different. If the extreme is
used once, next time don't use as much. Learn to not
only listen, but hear and communicate. Getting angry is
actually human, anger is a human emotion), because he
(Shechem) had wrought folly (a thoughtless or reckless
behavior) in Israel in lying with Jacob's daughter: which
thing ought not to be done.
8) And Hamor communed with them (Jacob and Dinah's

brothers), saying, The soul of my son Shechem longeth for your daughter: I pray you give her (Dinah) him to wife. (The King of Shalem wants Jacob to give Dinah to Shechem, his son, the Prince of Shalem to be Shechem's wife)

9) And make ye marriages with us, and give your daughters unto us, and take our daughters unto you. (Intercultural marriages)

10) And ye shall dwell with us: and the land shall be before you; dwell and trade ye therein, and get you possessions therein.

11) And Shechem said unto her father and unto her brethren, Let me find grace in your eyes, and what ye shall say unto me I will give.

12) Ask me never so much dowry and gift, and I will give according as ye shall say unto me: but give me the damsel to wife.

13) And the sons of Jacob answered Shechem and Hamor his father deceitfully, and said, because he had defiled Dinah their sister:

14) And they said unto them, We cannot do this thing, to give our sister to one that is uncircumcised; for that were a reproach unto us:

15) But in this will we consent unto you: If ye will be as we be, that every male of you be circumcised;

16) Then will we give our daughters unto you, and we will take your daughters to us, and we will dwell with you, and we will become one people.

17) But if ye will not hearken unto us, to be circumcised; then will we take our daughter, and we will be gone.

18) And their words pleased Hamor, and Shechem Hamor's son.

19) And the young man deferred not to do the thing, because he had delight in Jacob's daughter: and he was more honourable than all the house of his father.

20) And Hamor and Shechem his son came unto the gate

of their city, and communed with the men of their city, saying,

21) These men are peaceable with us; therefore let them dwell in the land, and trade therein; for the land, behold, it is large enough for them; let us take their daughters to us for wives, and let us give them our daughters.

22) Only herein will the men consent unto us for to dwell with us, to be one people, if every male among us be circumcised, as they are circumcised.

23) Shall not their cattle and their substance and every beast of their's be our's? only let us consent unto them, and they will dwell with us.

24) And unto Hamor and unto Shechem his son hearkened all that went out of the gate of his city; and every male was circumcised, all that went out of the gate of his city.

25) And it came to pass on the third day, when they were sore (the men were sore due to the circumcision), that two of the sons of Jacob, Simeon and Levi, Dinah's brethren, took each man his sword, and came upon the city boldly, and slew all the males.

26) And they (Dinah's brothers) slew Hamor and Shechem his son with the edge of the sword, and took Dinah out of Shechem's house, and went out.

27) The sons of Jacob came upon the slain, and spoiled the city, because they had defiled their sister.

28) They took their sheep, and their oxen, and their asses, and that which was in the city, and that which was in the field,

29) And all their wealth, and all their little ones, and their wives took they captive, and spoiled even all that was in the house.

30) And Jacob said to Simeon and Levi, Ye have troubled me to make me to stink among the inhabitants of the land, among the Canaanites and the Perizzites: and I being few in number, they shall gather themselves together against me, and slay me; and I shall be

destroyed, I and my house.

31) And they said, Should he deal with our sister as with an harlot? (Dinah's brother never heard a word or listened to a thing the King or Prince said, their anger blinded them. They had their minds made up before anyone even started talking and they conspired to kill the men)

(CONTINUED IN: HEAVENLY ANGEL LAY LAY EXPLAINS WHICH BIBLE TO READ, WHICH BIBLE NOT TO READ, AND WHY)

BIBLIOGRAPHY

1. Encarta ® World English Dictionary © & (P) 1998-2004 Microsoft Corporation. All rights reserved.

2. Merriam Webster's Collegiate Dictionary Tenth Edition (1993), United States of America.

3. The Holy Bible King James Version (1998), B. B. Kirkbride Bible Co., Inc. Indianapolis, IN..USA

www.ingramcontent.com/pod-product-compliance
Lightning Source LLC
LaVergne TN
LVHW091211080426
835509LV00006B/936